Mental Models for English/Language Arts

Grades 1–6

D1709940

Mental Models for English/Language Arts: Grades 1–6
102 pp.
ISBN-13 978-1-92922-954-3
ISBN-10 1-92922-954-2

1. Education   2. Sociology   3. Title

Bethanie H. Tucker, Ed.D. conceptualized and designed many of the mental models with contributions from Kim Ellis and Jennifer Ratka, as well as Jesse Conrad and Dan Shenk. Special thanks to the other consultants from **aha!** Process, Inc. who also participated in the effort.

Copy editing by Dan Shenk
Book design by Paula Nicolella
Cover design by ArtLink, Inc.

Mental Models for English/Language Arts

Grades 1–6

FOREWORD

The theory of mental models was first introduced by Kenneth Craik, a British philosopher and psychologist, in his 1943 book *The Nature of Explanation*. After his untimely death in a bicycle accident in 1945 (at age 31), the idea did not re-emerge in the literature until 1983 with the publication of Philip Johnson-Laird's book *Mental Models*.

Mental models have been defined as internalized, mental representations of things in the world—or internal symbols or representations of external phenomena. The representation that a person develops determines how he/she understands and interacts with the world. The more accurate the mental model, the more successful the interaction.

Mental models are believed to play a major part in cognition. When learners develop a more complete, accurate, and richer model of a particular domain, they become more competent in that domain. A teacher's main responsibility is to mediate students' learning so they formulate accurate, complete mental representations of abstract concepts as efficiently as possible.

The term *mental model*, as used in the field of education and in this workbook, is intended to describe strategies, visual representations, analogies, and stories that assist in the development of accurate internal symbols. Each mental model is designed to move the student closer to a deeper and richer understanding of the standards and abstract concepts necessary for success in the academic setting, as well as meaningful interaction with the world.

TABLE OF CONTENTS

Mental Models

Mental Models *(continued)*

Please note that the symbol appears in the top corner of the page at the beginning of each individual mental model.

INTRODUCTION

Mental Models for English/Language Arts

This workbook contains examples of mental models that teachers in Grades 1 through 6 can use in explaining English/language arts concepts.

The following information, taken from *Understanding Learning: the How, the Why, the What* by Dr. Ruby K. Payne, explains the characteristics and purposes of mental models.

- Mental models are how the mind holds abstract information, i.e., information that has no sensory representation.

- All subject areas or disciplines have their own blueprint or mental models.

- Mental models tell us what is and is not important in the discipline. They help the mind to sort.

- Mental models often explain the "why" of things working the way they do.

- Mental models tell the structure, purpose, or pattern of the discipline.

- Mental models are held in the mind as stories, analogies, movements, or two-dimensional drawings.

- Mental models "collapse" the amount of time it takes to teach/learn something.

- Mental models of a discipline are contained within the curriculum.

The mental models in this workbook involve four types: pictures, movement, stories, and analogies.

I.   Pictorial Mental Models

Many of the mental models contained in this workbook are two-dimensional drawings of three-dimensional or abstract concepts. Pictorial mental models enable the reader to grasp the concept and the instructor to explain it in less time than would be required through oral instructions alone.

Pictorial mental model for interrogative sentences

II.   Movement Mental Models

An example of a movement mental model in language arts is where students shape their hands to represent the parts of speech. As with all mental models, movement can reflect the structure, purpose, or a pattern in the discipline.

III.   Story Mental Models

Story mental models can range from cartoons that explain one concept or vocabulary word to chapter books that illustrate many related and interrelated concepts and generalizations. Several of the mental models in this workbook follow the story format, specifically that of cartoons.

IV.   Analogy Mental Models

An example of an analogy mental model could be the comparison of parts of a tree to elements of character development in literature:

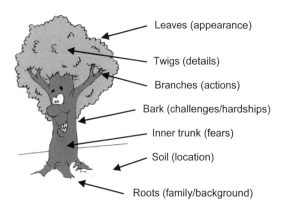

NOTE: Many mental models are a combination of two or more types.

Mental models tell the structure, purpose, or pattern of the discipline.

Purpose	To use structure and language to communicate
Structures	Literary genres (poetry, drama, fiction, nonfiction, etc.) Syntax of language (grammar) Written structures (persuasive, narrative, etc.) Phonemic structures of language (decoding) Word meaning (vocabulary) Written conventions of language (punctuation, spelling) Oral structures of language (speechmaking, dialogue) Structures of media (advertising, filmmaking, etc.)
Patterns (partial listing)	Literary structural patterns (characterization, story structure, point of view, etc.) Literary word patterns (rhythm, alliteration, etc.) Grammatical patterns (adverbial phrases, clauses, etc.) Logic and proof in written and oral persuasion Development of thesis and patterns of written text Patterns in the use of conventions, spelling, etc. Word-meaning patterns (root words, suffixes, verb tenses, etc.) Patterns in decoding (blends, diphthongs, short and long vowels, etc.) Patterns in spelling Common advertising appeals

Mental Models—the Ultimate Goal

The ultimate goal when working with mental models is for students to develop their own effective, personal mental models. Here is a step sheet to guide students in their progress.

Step Sheet for Student Development of Mental Models

1. Highlight or write out the concept for which you will develop a mental model.

2. Decide which type of mental model would be most effective for explaining the concept: pictorial, movement, story, analogy.

3. Take your time to develop your mental model in your mind.

4. Sketch, draw, or explain in a story your mental model.

5. Assess each component for efficiency, accuracy, and clarity.

6. Revise your mental model as your understanding of the concept grows.

Source: *Learning Structures* by Dr. Ruby K. Payne

Rubrics

Rubrics are essential tools in the identification of desired levels of student achievement and in setting standards.

Rubric Guidelines

- Rubrics must be simple and easy to understand. They are appropriate when the individual using them understands them. If a student is to use a rubric, he/she must be able to understand it.

- Student growth toward desired levels of achievement must be clear. The extent to which the student has met the standard must also be clear.

- Rubrics can be changed to meet various needs.

Developing a Rubric

1. Identify 3–5 criteria.

2. Set up a grid with numerical values: 1–4 is usually enough.

3. Identify what would be an excellent piece of work. That becomes a 4.

4. Work backward. Identify what would be a 3, a 2, and so on. What would be unacceptable? That becomes a 1.

Source: *Learning Structures*, by Dr. Ruby Payne

Mental Models

Mental Model for Long and Short Vowels

I'm the only vowel in town, and there's a consonant right behind me, so I feel shy. I think I'll make a quiet sound:

Ah! Now I'm not the only vowel in town. Even though my buddy, *e*, is silent, I feel brave with another vowel in the word with me. I think I'll make a long, brave sound:

www.ahaprocess.com

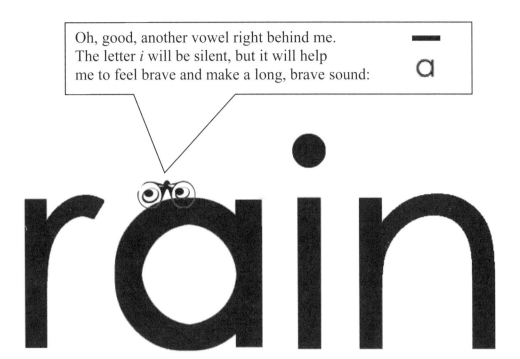

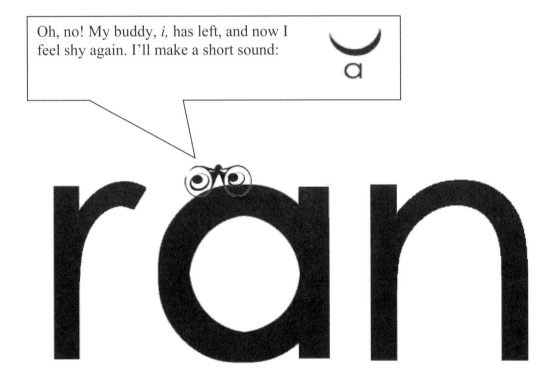

I don't know whether to be brave or shy now. I think I'll break this word into syllables …

locate

lo-cate

Now I know that in this syllable there is no consonant behind me to make me shy. So I'll be brave and make a long-*o* sound.

ō

Mental Model for Kinds of Sentences

Declarative—A declarative sentence **makes a statement** and ends with a period.

Example: The dog found his bone.

Interrogative—An interrogative sentence asks a question and ends with a question mark.

Example: How many students are in this room?

Imperative—An imperative sentence gives a command.

Example: Sit still and listen.

Exclamatory—An exclamatory sentence **shows strong feeling** and ends with an exclamation mark.

Example: This movie is scary!

Mental Model for Simple and Complex Sentences

Some twins are short; some twins are tall.

But they're still two different people.

Some sentences are short. Some sentences are long. But they are still two different sentences.

**He ran. He jumped.
She played. She won.**

Twins can be joined together with string.

Sentences can be joined together with conjunctions:

but, or, nor, for, so, yet, and

He ran, and he jumped.
She played, and she won.

Or, twins can simply hold hands,

just like semicolons joining two short sentences that are closely related but not joined.

He ran; he jumped.
She played; she won.

Mental Model for Paragraphs

Topic sentence

Supporting details

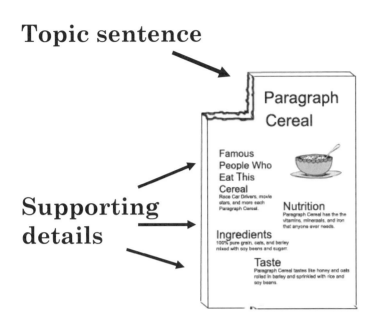

Example:

Cereal in My Pantry

    The first cereal in my pantry is Paragraph Cereal. It is very nutritious. And it is the favorite of many racecar drivers and movie stars. It is made of oats, wheat, and barley, and it tastes great.

    The second cereal in my pantry is #2 Paragraph Cereal. Many deep-sea divers eat this cereal every day ...

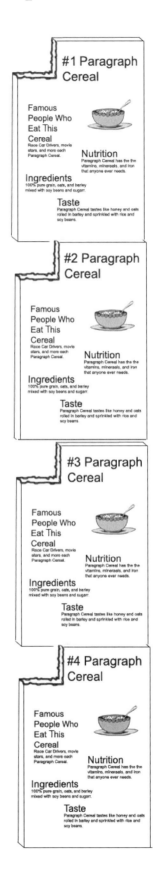

Movement Mental Model
for Parts of Speech

This is a picture frame,
  and it surrounds
Persons, places, things—
  we call them **nouns.**

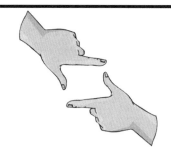

Adjectives describe nouns—
  a *funny, happy, dancing* clown.

(Move hands from inner [noun] to
    outer [adjective] position.)

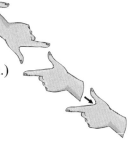

Verbs show action—
skip, hop, run,
  is, are, am, was,
and *has done.*

(Wiggle fingers.)

(Wiggle fingers, moving them from the inner [verb] to the outer [adverb] position.)

Adverbs describe verbs:
He *quickly* helps, she *gladly* serves.
Adverbs describe adjectives too—
A *really, truly,* comfy shoe.

Conjunctions are words
  (*and, but, when, or*)
That connect words:
  phrases, clauses, and more!

(Clasp hands together.)

Prepositions show relationships—
  in, with, from, to.
He's *in* the house, she's *on* vacation—
  by, at, for, through.

(Point in all directions.)

Interjections show emotion—
  Ugh! Oh! Wow!
And sometimes they show excitement—
  Hey! Ouch! Yow!

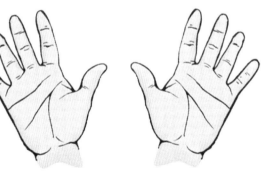

(Raise hands as if in surprise.)

Mental Model for Root Words, Prefixes, and Suffixes

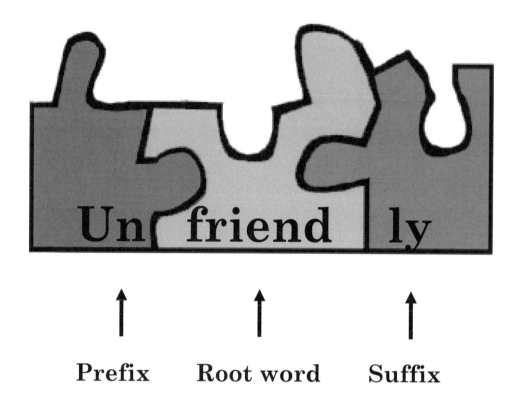

↑   ↑   ↑

Prefix   **Root word**   **Suffix**

When you add a new piece to a puzzle, it changes the meaning of the puzzle.

When you add a prefix to the beginning of a word, or a suffix to the end of a word, it changes the meaning of the word.

Mental Model for Steps of Writing Process

Step 1: Pre-Write (plan, brainstorm, gather ideas and materials)

Design ad
colors ?
restaurant
T-shirt
Deadline: May 30!!!!

Step 2: Write Draft

Ride by

sloppy

jos

Step 3: Revise

ete at

sloppy

jos

Step 4: Edit

Eat
ete at

S sloppy

Joe's
jos

Step 5: Publish

$18.95

Eat
at
Sloppy
Joe's

Pre-Writing—Steps to Follow

1. Gather pens, paper, computer, and other necessary materials.
2. Read the prompt or assignment.
3. Develop a planning page, including a timeline (planning backward from the day the assignment is due).
4. Get ideas on paper:
   - Brainstorm topics related to the prompt
   - Make a list
   - "Free write"
   - Research
   - Journal
   - Use graphic organizer, webbing, clustering, mapping
   - Make a topic chart

Writing the Draft—Steps to Follow

1. Look at the topics you have listed. Choose one and further research it.
2. Write, write, write. Revising and editing come later.
3. Before going to the next step, ask yourself if you have enough material to meet the requirements of the project. If not, repeat Steps 1 and 2.

Revising—Steps to Follow

1. Reread your draft. Using a different colored pen/pencil, check or mark your paper for overall continuity, such as:
   - Organization
   - Content
   - Audience
   - Point of view
   - Flow
   - Word choice

2. As you read, ask yourself such content questions as:
   - What else does the reader need to know?
   - Is the order of events logical?
   - Is there any unnecessary information?
   - Is the introduction catchy?
   - Do all sentences in each paragraph relate to the same topic?
   - Are all sentences complete?
3. Develop a rubric that lists categories for self- and peer-assessment of the revision step.
4. Have at least one other person read your paper and critique, using your rubric.
5. Rewrite your paper.

Editing—Steps to Follow

1. Get out your revised draft and planning sheet.
2. Develop an editing rubric with such headings as:
    - Spelling
    - Punctuation
    - Grammar
    - Subject/verb agreement
    - Capitalization
    - Sentence structure
    - Word usage

3. Reread Draft #2 and edit.
4. Find at least one peer to edit your paper, using your rubric.
5. Rewrite the paper, making corrections as marked or needed.

Publishing—Steps to Follow

1. Submit all stages of your paper in reverse order:

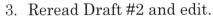

    - Final copy
    - Rough copies with evidence of revision and editing
    - Rubrics
    - Pre-writing

2. Enjoy the publication of your writing.

Mental Model for Sequence/Process

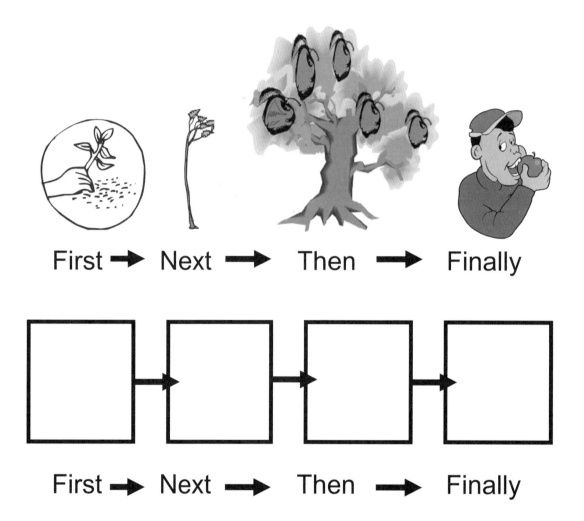

Mental Model for Developing Characters

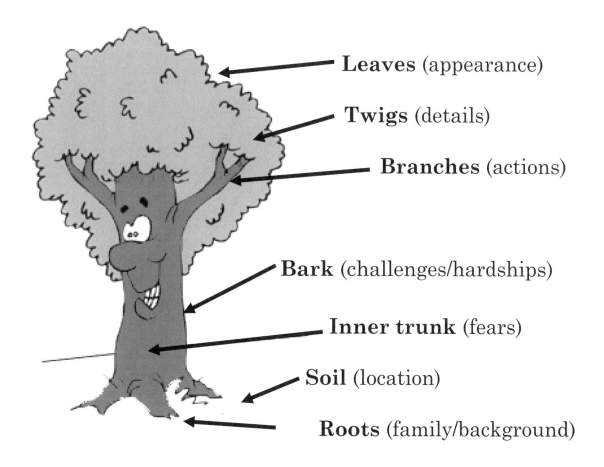

Leaves (appearance)

Twigs (details)

Branches (actions)

Bark (challenges/hardships)

Inner trunk (fears)

Soil (location)

Roots (family/background)

Mental Model for Fact or Opinion
in Written Text

The Sky Is Falling
by Chicken Little

**Published by
Little Chick Pub. Co.**

June 1, 1776

1. Who wrote it or said it?

2. Who is the publisher?

3. What is the point of view?

4. Is there any evidence?

5. When was it written?

Mental Model for Idioms

The early bird gets the worm

**Crocodile
tears**

Big Apple

Half-hearted

Idiom is Latin
for "personal" or private.

Cash cow

*Ha! Ha! Ha!
Ha! Ha!
Ha! Ha! Ha!*

A barrel of laughs

A hill of beans

Eat at

Oxymoron* Café

Menu:

The *biggest* little burger in town

Juicy dry turkey

Rare well-done steaks

Fresh frozen vegetables

Hot cold beverages

* a contradiction in terms

Mental Model for Irony

Irony is the use of language to express both a surface meaning and a different underlying meaning.

(There are several kinds of irony; this mental model shows only one of them.)

www.ahaprocess.com

Mental Model for Use of Multiple Sources

For my report I will use the gingerbread man and the dish running away with the spoon to show how things that are not alive can *come alive* in stories.

Mental Model for Genre

From the French word *gendre*, we get the words:

Gender
(Two "types" of human beings)

Male   Female

Genre
("Types" of literature)

Poetry, novels, short stories, biographies, fiction, autobiographies, movies, sitcoms, drama, myths, legends, science fiction, fantasy, folk tales, mystery, historical fiction ...

Mental Model for Genres—Magic Pencils

Hi, I'm a TV announcer. Use my magic pencil to write any kind of TV show: dramatic programs, news shows, situation comedies, etc.

Use my magic pencil to write scripts for video games.

Use my magic pencil for writing drama.

Mental Model for Story Structure

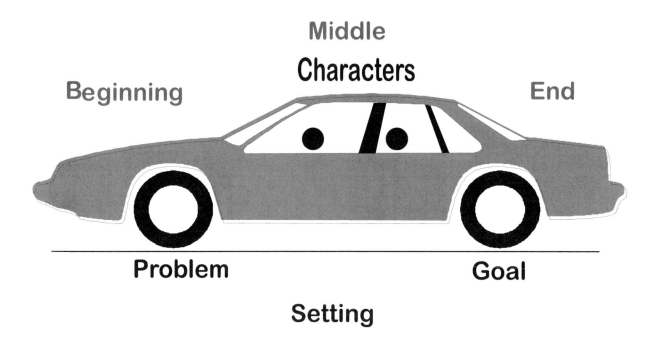

Mental Model for Reading and Understanding Literature

The genre, or "kind" of literature, determines the characters, setting, and plot of the story.

The moral, or message, moves the story along.

Mental Model for Author's Purpose

Mental Model for Main Idea

Mental Model for Poetic Devices

I don't want to find examples of poetic devices for homework. I'd rather read nursery rhymes instead.

I can't find an example of *alliteration*—the repetition of initial consonant sounds. So I'll read *Peter Piper picked a peck of pickled peppers* instead.

And I don't understand **assonance**—the repetition of vowel sounds—but I love the sound of *Moses supposes his toeses are roses, but Moses supposes erroneously.*

I don't care about **imagery,** but I love to read, *Twinkle, Twinkle, Little Star.* I can almost see the stars twinkling.

And **metaphor**—a comparison of two objects— what does that mean? I'll read this poem ...
If all the world were paper,
And all the sea were ink ...

And what is **meter**? I don't know, but I like to clap my hands to the beat of *Humpty Dumpty.*

Onomatopoeia—the use of words that imitate sound. I don't get it. I think I'll read *"Pop" Goes the Weasel.*

I've never heard of **personification**—when animals, ideas, or inanimate objects are given human traits or abilities.

I'll just read *Hey, diddle diddle, the cat and the fiddle, the cow jumped over the moon; the little dog laughed to see such sport, and the dish ran away with the spoon.*

Repetition—the repeating of words, phrases, lines, or stanzas. That doesn't sound very exciting.

I think I'll read *London Bridge is falling down, falling down, falling down.*

I don't care about **rhyme**—the similarity of ending sounds in words—but listen to this:

Little Jack Horner sat in a corner.

Now that has a good sound to it.

And I don't understand **rhyme scheme**—the sequence in which the rhyme occurs. The first end sound is "a," the second is "b," etc.

I'd rather read
*Jack and **Jill** went up the **hill***
*To fetch a pail of **water***
*Jack fell **down** and broke his **crown***
*And Jill came tumbling **after.***

I love all those rhyming words in the middle of the sentences!

And what in the world is a **simile**? This says a simile is a comparison of two objects using "like" or "as." I don't get it, but I love this line:

Mary had a little lamb; its fleece was white as snow.

Alliteration—the repetition of initial consonant sounds. *Peter Piper picked a peck of pickled peppers.*

Assonance—the repetition of vowel sounds. *Moses supposes his toeses are roses, but Moses supposes erroneously.*

Imagery—words or phrases that appeal to any sense or any combination of senses. *Twinkle, Twinkle, Little Star.*

Metaphor—a comparison of two objects in order to give clearer meaning to one of them. *If all the world were paper, and all the sea were ink ...*

Meter—a pattern of stressed and unstressed syllables. *Humpty Dumpty sat on a wall.*

Onomatopoeia—words that imitate sounds. *Pop! Goes the weasel!*

Personification—a figure of speech that gives human traits or abilities to animals, ideas, or inanimate objects. *And the dish ran away with the spoon.*

Repetition—the repeating of words, phrases, lines, or stanzas. *London Bridge is falling down, falling down, falling down.*

Rhyme—the similarity of ending sounds in words. *Little Jack Horner sat in a corner.*

Rhyme scheme—the sequence in which the rhyme occurs. The first end sound is represented as the letter "a," the second is "b," etc. *Jack and Jill went up the hill.*

Simile—a comparison of two objects using "like" or "as." *Its fleece was white as snow.*

Mental Model for Author's Voice

Mental Model for Tone

Literary Technique Poetry

Figurative Language

I don't use figurative language:
Metaphors and similes;
I just use teenage slanguage …
It's all I really need.

I tell my friends they're dumb as dirt—
And other teenage slanguage;
Or I might say that words can hurt,
But I don't use *figurative* language!

Simile

You smell like a rose to me.
Hey, I wrote a simile!

Spring's as brilliant as my mother.
Look at that! I wrote another.

Similes are like a game:
Comparing ideas that aren't the same,
Connecting them with *as* and *like*,
To decorate the words you write.

You are nothing like a rose
'Til your aroma's on my nose!

Hyperbole

"You say I run like lightning. But how in blazes could that be?"
        "It's an exaggeration … just hyperbole."
"You say I'm older than the hills. You are so mean to me!"
        "I've told you a million times: I use hyperbole!"

I'd work an eternity …
To come up with good hyperbole!

Personification

Hey, diddle diddle, the cat and the fiddle, the cow jumped over the moon;
The little dog laughed to see such sport, and the dish ran away with the spoon.

Hey, diddle diddle! Cats can't play fiddle, and spoons run in your imagination;
So when cats and spoons act like people, we call this "personification."

Alliteration

Mary had a little lamb, little lamb, little lamb.
Did you hear the two *s* sounds? That's alliteration!

Peter Piper picked a peck of pickled peppers
And rolled a red rubber baby buggy home.

It's not just consonants of which alliteration's made;
Here's a vowel example: apt alliteration's artful aid.

So if you'd like to try a tongue-twister creation,
Just listen to your leaning and launch into alliteration.

Metaphor

Metaphors can make us think:
Is time really money?
Or do we just compare two things—
To make our language sunny?

A metaphor compares two things,
But it's not a simile;
Life's a beach, your mind's a sponge,
And my family is a tree.

When something described *is* something more,
That, my friend, is a metaphor!

Onomatopoeia

Bang, bark, zap, and ting:
They all sound like what they mean.

Pow, pop, snarl, and clang:
Onomatopoeias give language a *bang*!

Flashback

A flashback to my childhood
Can help me better guess
Why I behave the way I do—
And what I might do next!

Flashbacks in a made-up story
Can help us all to know
What characters can still recall—
And where the plot might go.

When characters have flashbacks
In dreams or just narration,
We get the background of their plight
And learn their motivation.

Literary Forms Poetry

Myth

Why do leaves change colors? Could they be a gift
The fairies gave to autumn? Or is this just a myth?

For generations myriad myths have been handed down
To tell us why the sky is blue—or why the world is
      round.

The Greek god Zeus is just a myth (same goes for all the rest);
Lots of groups explain with myths, but I like the Greek ones best.

Didactic Literature

Didactic books give instructions 'cause they teach and teach;
But non-didactics might best describe a sunset on the beach.

Didactic writing makes a point—whether it's welcome or not,
While non-didactics could well describe a flower in a pot.

Political or moral, didactics send a message;
Non-didactics might be just a story or a passage.

Allegory

Metaphors are short and sweet,
While allegories are longer;
Worried that your points are weak?
Allegories make them stronger.

Allegories are stories and poems
(Extended metaphors);
They're both literal and figurative—
With characters, plots, and more!

Mental Model for Sorting
Important/Unimportant Information

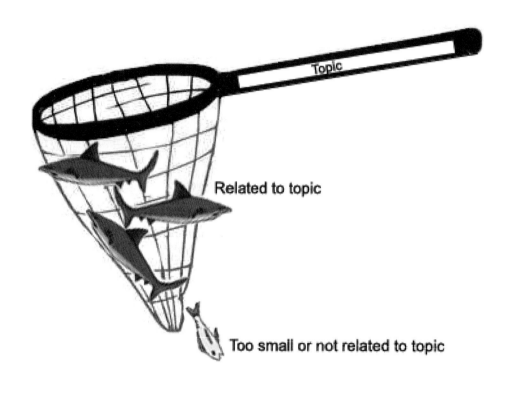

Draw a shark shape around the most important information in each paragraph.

www.ahaprocess.com

Mental Model for Descriptive/Topical Writing

Write a topic on each finger;
sort information by writing
details on fingers.

Mental Model for Sequence/How-To

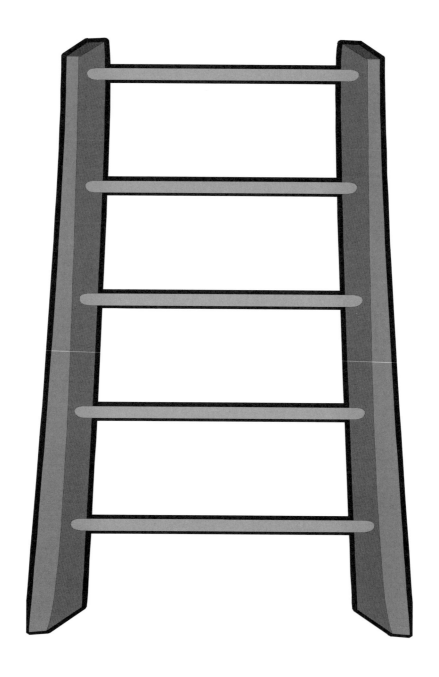

Mental Model for Persuasive Writing

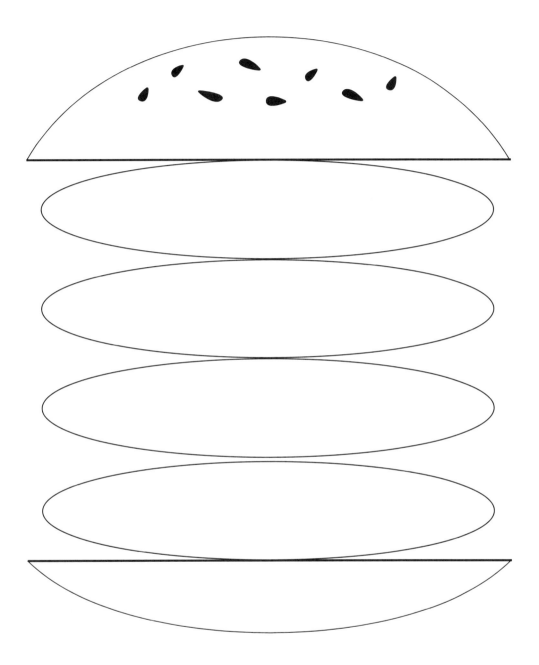

The top bun represents the thesis statement.

Each filler represents supporting details.

The bottom bun represents the restatement or summary.

Mental Model for Organizing Research Folder

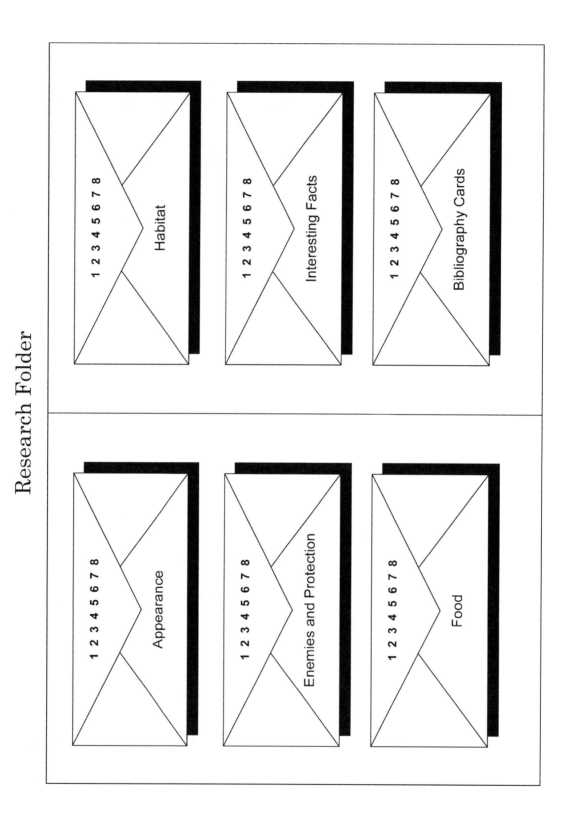

Mental Model for Organization for Writing Example—Novels

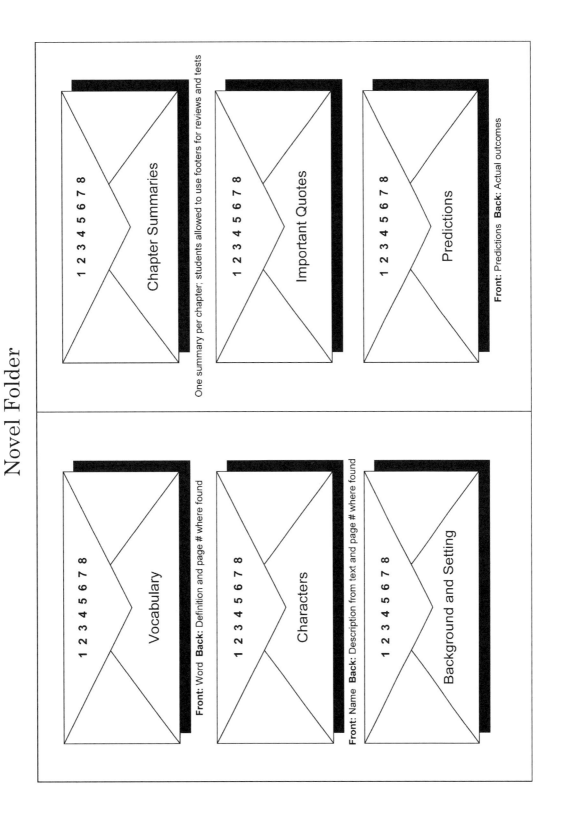

Mental Model for Initiating Conversation

So, how do you like our school?
Did you say you have two brothers?
Where did you live before moving here?
I think I heard you say you like math.

Bobby, what are you doing?

I'm practicing initiating conversation with the new girl at school.

I'm *asking questions,* *restating,* and *requesting information.*

Mental Model for Listening

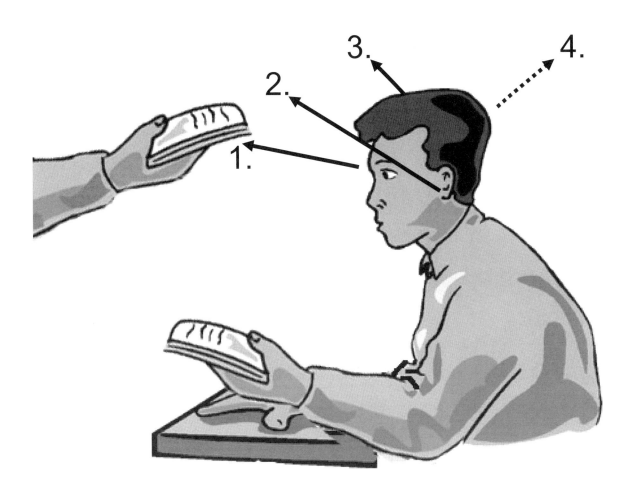

1. Look at speaker.
2. Pay attention to content, not to how he/she stands, etc.
3. Ask yourself questions about the content.
4. Avoid distractions.

Mental Model for Identifying Fact and Opinion in Spoken English

Mental Model for Listening to Media

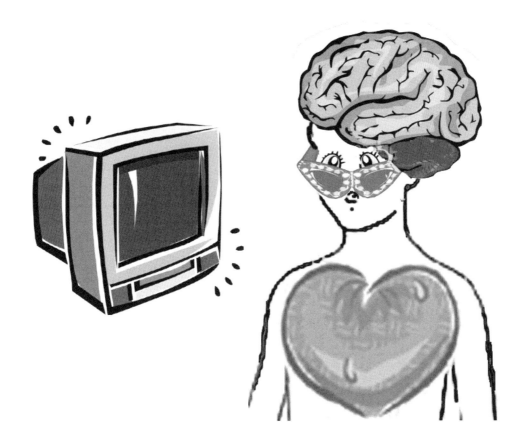

The media try to make you (1) ***think,*** (2) ***watch*** (or listen), and (3) ***feel with your heart.***

The media attempt to (1) ***persuade,*** (2) ***entertain,*** and (3) ***appeal to emotions.***

Rubrics and Step Sheets

LISTENING SKILLS RUBRICS

Standard: Make inferences and predictions
- Demonstrate proficiency in listening skills, including focusing attention, avoiding listening emotionally, and avoiding distractions

Steps for student to follow:
1. Memorize the four points of listening.
2. Rehearse each point before listening to a speaker.

Four Points of Listening Rubric

Criterion	4 Exceeds Standard	3 Meets Standard	2 Is Below Standard	1 Does Not Meet Standard
Make inferences and predictions	Looks at speaker; pays attention to content, not how he/she stands, etc.; asks oneself about content; and avoids distractions	Can infer speaker's message; remains focused	Can use eye contact; responds to speaker's tone and voice	Is easily distracted and cannot respond to tone and voice; listens emotionally and does not focus

www.ahaprocess.com

Standard: Make inferences and predictions
- Differentiate fact from opinion on topics or issues presented by speaker

Steps for student to follow:
1. Study the mental model to determine why the listener considers the first three comments to be opinion.
2. Determine why the listener determines the four comments to be fact.

Fact and Opinion Rubric

Criterion	4 Exceeds Standard	3 Meets Standard	2 Is Below Standard	1 Does Not Meet Standard
Make inferences and predictions	Differentiates fact and opinion about topics presented by speakers and broadcast media; is able to give examples of fact and opinion	Is able to infer speaker's overall implied message as fact or opinion	Is not able to consistently differentiate between fact and opinion	Cannot differentiate fact and opinion about topics presented by speakers or broadcast media

Standard: Identify speaker attitude and point of view
- Identify strategies used by speakers and broadcast media, such as entertaining, persuading, and appealing to emotions

Steps for student to follow:
1. Study the three strategies used by speakers and broadcast media pictured in the mental model.
2. Try to determine the intent of speakers, TV shows, and advertisements.
3. Share with a friend.

Point of View Rubric

Criterion	4 Exceeds Standard	3 Meets Standard	2 Is Below Standard	1 Does Not Meet Standard
Identify speaker attitude and point of view	Understands and identifies strategies used by various speakers and broadcast media, including persuasion, entertainment, and appeal to emotions	Demonstrates understanding of speaker's purpose and message; is able to interpret speaker's message and purposes	Demonstrates understanding of speaker's attitude toward topic or purpose	Cannot demonstrate understanding of speaker's attitude toward topic

Cumulative Listening Skills Rubric

Criteria	4 Exceeds Standard	3 Meets Standard	2 Is Below Standard	1 Does Not Meet Standard
Identify main ideas and supporting details from spoken English	Can critique accuracy of spoken message and can identify main idea and more than two supporting details in spoken message	Can identify main idea and one or two supporting details in spoken message	Can identify main points in spoken message	Demonstrates minimal comprehension of spoken English
Follow spoken directions	Can clarify spoken directions and can follow spoken directions to successfully complete task	Can follow most spoken directions to complete task	Can follow simple spoken directions to complete task with two-step directions or less	Cannot follow two-step spoken directions to complete task
Understand spoken English in social contexts	Can give examples to clarify points made by others and can ask questions about message	Can respond to messages by asking questions and clarifying main points made by others	Can understand messages from others by repeating main points	Cannot understand greetings, questions, or directions
Identify main ideas and techniques used in broadcast media	Can identify techniques used and critique intent of broadcast media	Can identify intent of broadcast media	Can identify main points of broadcast media	Cannot correctly identify intent or main ideas of broadcast media
Identify speaker point of view	Can identify strategies used by speakers and broadcast media, such as persuasion, entertainment, and appeal to emotions	Can identify speaker's messages and purposes	Can use eye contact	Cannot demonstrate understanding of speaker's feelings

SPEAKING SKILLS RUBRICS

Standard: Engage in social conversations for personal enjoyment, expression, and exchange of ideas
- Initiate social conversations by asking questions, restating, and requesting information

Steps for student to follow:
1. Study the mental model and memorize the four ways to initiate conversation.
2. Rehearse each step just before initiating conversation with someone.
3. Practice with a friend or another student in your class. Try to use each of the four ways to initiate conversation.

Initiating Conversation Rubric

Criterion	4 Exceeds Standard	3 Meets Standard	2 Is Below Standard	1 Does Not Meet Standard
Engage in social conversations for personal enjoyment, expression, and exchange of ideas	Shows proficiency in listening skills; effectively utilizes all four methods of initiating conversation	Demonstrates average listening skills; can use three of four methods of initiating conversation	Listening skills need improvement; is able to use two of four methods of initiating conversation	Listening skills are poor; is not able to effectively use methods of initiating conversation

Standard: Use spoken English in socially acceptable ways
- Use idiomatic expressions appropriately

Steps for student to follow:
1. Study the idiomatic expressions in the mental model.
2. Check the expressions that you have heard.
3. In a notebook make a list of idiomatic expressions that you hear.
4. Research these expressions to determine their origins.

Idioms Rubric

Criterion	4 Exceeds Standard	3 Meets Standard	2 Is Below Standard	1 Does Not Meet Standard
Use spoken English in socially acceptable ways	Uses idiomatic expressions appropriately and colorfully	Recognizes and uses idiomatic expressions	Recognizes idiomatic expressions	Does not recognize idiomatic expressions

READING SKILLS RUBRICS

Standard: Understand literary patterns
- Understand effect of genre on characters, setting, and plot
- Understand role of moral in movement of characters, settings, and plot

Steps for student to follow:
1. Study the mental model and decide how characters, plot, setting, and moral reflect genre.
2. Read a story. While reading, identify the characters, plot, and setting.
3. Then determine the moral.
4. Finally, decide how the moral helps to move the characters, plot, and setting.

Literary Patterns Rubric

Criterion	4 Exceeds Standard	3 Meets Standard	2 Is Below Standard	1 Does Not Meet Standard
Read and identify main and supporting ideas	Can identify and describe interrelationship of characters, plot, and setting Can describe how moral "moves" story along Can explain how genre determines characters, plot, and setting	Can identify characters, plot, and setting Can explain how moral moves story along and how characters, plot, and setting reflect genre	Can identify characters, plot and setting Can identify and explain moral	Can identify characters, plot, and setting Cannot explain relationships among genre, characters, plot, setting, and moral

www.ahaprocess.com

Standard: Recognize and analyze styles of various genres
- Identify purpose, style, and ideas of author

Steps for student to follow:
1. Study the mental model and memorize the three possible purposes that authors have in mind when they write.
2. Determine the author's purpose of each text, book, short story, etc., that you read.

Author's Purpose Rubric

	4	3	2	1
Criterion	**Exceeds Standard**	**Meets Standard**	**Is Below Standard**	**Does Not Meet Standard**
Analyze author's purpose	Analyzes texts and accurately determines major and minor purpose(s) of author in grade-level and some above-grade-level documents	Analyzes texts and accurately determines major purpose of author in most grade-level documents	Can identify major purpose of author in some documents that are at or below grade level	Cannot identify major purpose of author in grade-level documents; is able to identify purpose of below-grade-level documents

Standard: Demonstrate comprehension of main ideas and supporting details
- Identify main idea and supporting details of text

Steps for student to follow:
1. Study the mental model and think about what the older boy said the book was about (the main idea) and evidence (supporting ideas).
2. Decide in your mind why he doesn't realize he has completed his homework.
3. Review stories you have read in the past. Discuss a main idea and supporting detail from a story.

Main Idea Rubric

	4	3	2	1
Criterion	**Exceeds Standard**	**Meets Standard**	**Is Below Standard**	**Does Not Meet Standard**
Read and identify main and supporting ideas	Identifies main and supporting ideas in above-grade-level text	Identifies main and supporting ideas in grade-level text	Identifies main idea in grade-level text; attempts to identify supporting details	Cannot identify main idea or supporting idea of grade-level text; identifies main idea in below-grade-level text

Standard: Read for research purposes
- Evaluate and synthesize information from multiple sources for various research purposes

Steps for student to follow:
1. Study the mental model.
2. Determine how the student has synthesized information from two sources for use in his/her presentation.

Reading for Research Rubric

Criterion	4 Exceeds Standard	3 Meets Standard	2 Is Below Standard	1 Does Not Meet Standard
Read for research purposes	Reads, evaluates, and synthesizes information from multiple sources for various purposes, including presentations, reports, and projects	Collects and organizes information from multiple sources for various purposes, including presentations, reports, and projects	Collects and organizes information from one source other than textbook for various purposes	Collects information from textbook only for presentation or report purposes

Standard: Analyze style and form of genre
- Identify poetic devices

Steps for student to follow:
1. Study the mental model to determine how each speech bubble illustrates a poetic device.
2. Read the cumulative list explaining poetic devices. Think of another example to illustrate each.
3. Find additional examples as you read poetry for class or for pleasure.

Poetic Devices Rubric

Criterion	4 Exceeds Standard	3 Meets Standard	2 Is Below Standard	1 Does Not Meet Standard
Analyze style and form of genre	Analyzes poetry and identifies multiple poetic devices; is able to define devices	Recognizes examples of poetic devices and attempts to explain definition of device	Recognizes some examples of poetic devices	Cannot recognize or give example of more than one or two poetic devices

www.ahaprocess.com

Standard: Identify literary devices, including oxymoron

Steps for student to follow:
1. Student the mental model to determine how the items on the menu are examples of oxymoron.
2. Think of your own example of an oxymoron.
3. Find additional examples as you read poetry for class or for pleasure.

Oxymoron Rubric

Criterion	4 Exceeds Standard	3 Meets Standard	2 Is Below Standard	1 Does Not Meet Standard
Analyze style and form of genre	Analyzes and identifies examples of oxymoron; is able to create original examples	Recognizes and analyzes some examples of oxymoron	Recognizes a few examples of oxymoron	Cannot recognize or give example of more than one oxymoron

Standard: Identify literary devices, including irony

Steps for student to follow:
1. Study the mental model and compare the actual comments of the characters with the "underlying" meanings.
2. Write a definition of irony in your own words.
3. Search for additional examples of irony in other texts.

Irony Rubric

Criterion	4 Exceeds Standard	3 Meets Standard	2 Is Below Standard	1 Does Not Meet Standard
Identify literary devices, including irony	Identifies irony in texts Uses irony in written and oral work	Understands ironic comments in mental model cartoon and identifies irony in texts	Understands ironic comments in mental model cartoon	Cannot identify or give example of irony

Standard: Identify author's voice

Steps for student to follow:
1. Study the mental model for an understanding of author's voice.
2. Determine the author's voice in texts, books, shorts stories, poems, etc., that you read.

Author's Voice Rubric

Criterion	4 Exceeds Standard	3 Meets Standard	2 Is Below Standard	1 Does Not Meet Standard
Identify author's voice in written text	Analyzes text and correctly determines author's voice; can identify author's voice in and above grade-level text	Understands that various texts reflect different voices; can identify author's voice in grade-level text	Understands that various texts reflect differing emotions of author; can identify author's voice in below-grade-level text	Understands that various texts reflect differing emotions of author but cannot recognize author's voice

Standard: Identify author's tone
- Recognize how author's tone contributes to literary effect

Steps for student to follow:
1. Study the mental model and determine the meaning of tone.
2. Decide how tone can be detected in written texts.
3. Read a text and identify the author's tone.
4. Analyze various texts for author's tone.

Author's Tone Rubric

Criterion	4 Exceeds Standard	3 Meets Standard	2 Is Below Standard	1 Does Not Meet Standard
Recognize how author's tone contributes to literary effect	Interprets author's tone and describes effect of tone on text	Identifies tone in grade-level text; attempts to interpret effect of tone on text	Identifies author's tone in text at or below grade level	Cannot identify author's point of view or tone in text

Standard: Identify styles of various genres
- Identify elements of literary techniques

Steps for student to follow:
1. Read each poem.
2. For each poem, determine how the content illustrates the term being defined.
3. Search for additional examples of each literary technique in other texts.
4. Create your own example of each term.

Reading Skills Rubric

Criterion	4 Exceeds Standard	3 Meets Standard	2 Is Below Standard	1 Does Not Meet Standard
Identify elements of literary techniques	Identifies multiple examples of various elements in variety of texts; creates original examples	Identifies examples of literary techniques in grade-level text; creates examples	Explains how poems illustrate literary techniques; cannot create examples	Cannot explain literary techniques illustrated in poems; cannot create examples

Standard: Identify style of genre
- Understand literary forms, such as myths, historical fiction, fables, and biographies

Steps for student to follow:
1. Read each poem.
2. Determine how the content of the poems illustrate the term being defined.
3. Think about a piece of literature you have read. Try to see which poem best describes that piece of literature.
4. Search for additional examples of each literary form in other texts.

Literary Forms Rubric

Criterion	4 Exceeds Standard	3 Meets Standard	2 Is Below Standard	1 Does Not Meet Standard
Identify literary forms	Explains characteristics of multiple literary forms Identifies multiple examples of various literary forms	Identifies multiple examples of various literary forms	Identifies examples of basic literary forms, such as poetry, myths, and tall tales	Cannot identify examples of literary forms

WRITING SKILLS RUBRICS

Standard: Demonstrate comprehension of main ideas and supporting details
- Use grammatical writing conventions accurately

Steps for student to follow:
1. Study the mental model and determine the proper use of semicolons and conjunctions.
2. Practice each step many times prior to using the strategy while taking tests.

Grammatical Conventions Rubric

Criterion	4 Exceeds Standard	3 Meets Standard	2 Is Below Standard	1 Does Not Meet Standard
Use grammatical writing conventions accurately	Uses punctuation and conjunctions to produce complex sentences without run-on or fragmented sentences	Frequently uses conjunctions and punctuation correctly; may have three or fewer errors	Uses conjunctions correctly; may have more than three errors in punctuation	Misuses punctuation Writes using run-on and fragmented sentences

Standard: Write stories and other narratives that employ logical sequence of events

Steps for student to follow:
1. Study the mental model.
2. Fill in the appropriate steps in the sequence with the directions given in the box.
3. Use the sequence mental model as a guide for future writing that requires sequencing of events.

Sequencing Rubric

Criterion	4 Exceeds Standard	3 Meets Standard	2 Is Below Standard	1 Does Not Meet Standard
Write stories and other narratives that employ logical sequence of events	Writes for variety of purposes using logical and clearly delineated sequences of events with details and transitions	Writes for variety of purposes using accurate sequence of events	Writes short stories using logical overall sequence of events	Writes using illogical sequencing

www.ahaprocess.com

Standard: Use various types of writing for specific purposes

Steps for student to follow:
1. Study the mental model.
2. In order to match the picture with the article, fill in the mental model sheet.
3. Use the sequence mental model as a guide for writing newspaper articles.

Article Writing Rubric

Criterion	4 Exceeds Standard	3 Meets Standard	2 Is Below Standard	1 Does Not Meet Standard
Use various types of writing for specific purposes	Writes for variety of purposes, including newspaper reports answering questions who, what, why, how, when, and where	Writes for variety of purposes, including newspaper reports; answers four of six questions	Writes in differing forms for differing purposes; answers three or fewer questions	Does not alter writing to match purpose; does not answer questions

Standard: Use various types of writing for specific purposes
- Write compare/contrast compositions

Steps for student to follow:
1. Study the mental model and determine how the two characters pictured are alike and how they are different.
2. Brainstorm some words/phrases to fill in the pumpkins.
3. Use the mental model concept as a guide for writing in the form of comparisons/contrasts.

Compare and Contrast Rubric

	4	3	2	1
Criteria	**Exceeds Standard**	**Meets Standard**	**Is Below Standard**	**Does Not Meet Standard**
Stay on topic	Consistently stays on topic Writes effectively for purpose/mode Addresses topic/purpose in concise manner	May have slight inconsistency but is holistically consistent Writes for correct mode/purpose Addresses topic	May have slight inconsistency but is holistically consistent Addresses topic some of time Writes for correct purpose/mode	Addresses topic/purpose in skeletal or general manner Drifts from topic Writes for wrong purpose and mode
Organization and structure	Well-planned and organized so that topic sentences and transitions flow from one paragraph to next Paragraphs are used to discuss similarities and differences Well-developed introductory and concluding elements that connect to one another	Generally well-organized and clear enough to understand ideas presented Paragraphs indicate use of transition from one thought to another Evidence of introductory and concluding elements	Organization apparent Some gaps, rambling, and inconsistencies Gives two similarities and two differences but may be all in one paragraph Has introduction and may have conclusion	Lacks adequate number of similarities/ differences Lacks organization No obvious transitions from one topic/paragraph to another

(continued on next page)

Compare and Contrast Rubric *(continued)*

Criteria	4 **Exceeds Standard**	3 **Meets Standard**	2 **Is Below Standard**	1 **Does Not Meet Standard**
Development	Elaborates in variety of ways (i.e., simile, example, anecdote, etc.) Uses at least three methods of elaboration to support single idea	Uses at least two methods of elaboration to support a single idea (simile, example, anecdote, etc.) Slight repetition/ digression may occur	Adequate number of ideas provided Minimal elaboration of ideas	No elaboration of ideas Attempts elaboration by explaining idea with only one sentence
Language control	Consistent control of language Adheres to writing conventions Few, if any, errors in spelling, grammar, mechanics Varies sentence structure, including compound and complex sentences Rich, sophisticated, and vivid word choice	Exhibits control of language Occasional errors in spelling, grammar, mechanics, writing, conventions Some variation in sentence structure Effective word choice using at or above grade-level vocabulary	Some errors in spelling, grammar, mechanics, writing conventions Awkward or simple sentences Limited word choice Some sentence fragments or run-on sentences Effective word choice using grade-level vocabulary	Numerous fragments or run-on sentences Illogical, confusing sentences Numerous errors in spelling, grammar, mechanics, writing conventions Ineffective word choice; may frequently use words from below grade level
Special features *	* To be added at teacher's discretion—first draft			

Standard: Use various types of writing for specific purposes; gather evaluate, and synthesize data from variety of sources

Steps for student to follow:
(Use this mental model to sort information for writing a research paper.)
1. Determine the subtopics of your major research topic.
2. Write one subtopic on each envelope of your *Research Folder*.
3. Research your topic using a variety of sources.
4. Quote or paraphrase information from your research on index cards and file each card in the appropriate envelope.
5. For each source you use, write the bibliographical information on a separate index card and file it in the *Bibliography Card* envelope.
6. Cross off a number across the top of the envelope into which each index card is filed.
7. When all eight (may vary) numbers have been checked off a particular envelope, you possibly have enough information on that topic for your final paper.
8. If you find additional information on a subtopic for which all numbers have been checked off, you may substitute the new information by removing a previously filed card.
9. When all envelopes have been completed, gather the cards from the first envelope and use the information on them to write your introductory thesis paragraph.
10. Continue until information from all index cards has been used or discarded.
11. Turn in the folder, with index cards filed, with your completed paper.

Research/Novel Folder Rubric

Criteria	4 Exceeds Standard	3 Meets Standard	2 Is Below Standard	1 Does Not Meet Standard
Use various types of writing for specific purposes **Gather, evaluate, and synthesize data from variety of sources**	Gathers data from variety of sources Evaluates data and categories accurately Synthesizes data into logical, easy-to-follow report Writes report appropriate to audience	Required number of sources used Data accurately categorized Report lacks detail and explanation	Required number of sources used, though some not categorized correctly Report lacks detail and/or some information not logical	Fewer than required number of sources used Some data not categorized correctly Report not logically arranged

www.ahaprocess.com

Standard: Employ wide range of strategies in writing

Descriptive Writing Rubric

	4 Exceeds Standard	3 Meets Standard	2 Is Below Standard	1 Does Not Meet Standard
Criteria				
Stay on topic	Presents description in detailed and logical order (sequential, topical)	Stays on topic Presents description in order (sequential, topical)	Addresses topic and purpose in disorganized fashion Occasionally drifts	Does not address topic Responses are not descriptive
Organization and structure	Has introduction, body, and conclusion Shows strong sense of organizational strategy within paragraphs	Has introduction, body, and conclusion Paragraphs indicate use of transition from one thought to another	Shows some sense of organization Some gaps, rambling, and inconsistencies	Lacks organization Rambles Major gaps
Language control	Consistent control of language Few, if any errors in spelling, grammar, word choice Varied sentence construction Excellent use of adjectives, adverbs	Complete sentences Some variation in sentence structure Occasional errors in spelling, grammar, and word choice	Awkward or simple sentences Some errors in spelling, grammar, and word choice Little use of adjectives and adverbs	Incomplete sentences Illogical, confusing sentences Repeated errors in spelling, grammar, and word choice
Support and elaboration	Specific elaboration, which is highly descriptive and may include metaphors, similes, allusions, etc. Rich, unique word choice Vividly addresses sensory details using four or more senses	Moderate elaboration Effective word choice Addresses details through two or three senses	Some elaboration Limited word choice Addresses details through one sense	Insufficient elaboration to support description Minimal word choice Fails to address sensory details

Standard: Employ wide range of strategies in writing

How-To Writing Rubric

Criteria	4 Exceeds Standard	3 Meets Standard	2 Is Below Standard	1 Does Not Meet Standard
Stay on topic	Directions are clearly stated, developed, and related throughout Remains highly focused	Directions are clearly stated and related throughout Remains focused	Directions are stated and related throughout Topic is somewhat related Occasionally drifts off topic	Directions are unclear, confusing Addresses topic in skeletal manner
Organization and structure	Clear sense of order and completeness Sequences logically Appropriate/ sophisticated transitions Consistent and effective organization	Has introduction, body, and conclusion Most points logically sequenced Some transitions Occasional gaps in organization	Apparent organization and sequence Some inconsistencies Uneven use of transitions Has introduction and conclusion	No organization evident Much confusion and many inconsistencies Rambles and is repetitive Drifts off topic

(continued on next page)

How-To Writing Rubric *(continued)*

Criteria	4 — Exceeds Standard	3 — Meets Standard	2 — Is Below Standard	1 — Does Not Meet Standard
Language control	Shows consistent control of language Few, if any, grammatical errors Varied sentence structure	Exhibits control of language Some errors, such as capitalization, punctuation, minor spelling errors, incorrect subject/verb agreement Some variation in sentence structure	Awkward, simple, and/or fragmented sentences Errors in spelling, capitalization, and punctuation, and subject/verb agreement	Incomplete sentences Illogical, confusing sentences Major and/or repeated errors in spelling usage and word choice
Support and elaboration	Process is presented effectively through sequential steps Elaboration for each step uses explanation, example, or detail with at least three accurate and complete examples/details/explanation Clear and convincing Rich, unusual, creative, and/or vivid choice of words	Process is presented partially through sequential steps Effective word choice Sufficient support providing two or more accurate and complete examples	Minimal elaboration Limited word choice Support is attempted; may provide two incomplete examples or less than two	Insufficient elaboration Few or no supporting points Inadequate word choice
Reader appeal	Fluent Interesting, intriguing Creative, unusual Flows naturally	Fairly typical Somewhat interesting Flows with minor gaps	Ordinary May have some gaps that lead toward confusion for reader	Not interesting Confusing Awkward

Standard: Employ wide range of strategies in writing and use different writing-process elements appropriately to communicate with different audiences for variety of purposes

The Writing Process Rubric

Criteria	4 Exceeds Standard	3 Meets Standard	2 Is Below Standard	1 Does Not Meet Standard
Stay on topic	Remains on topic with logic Logical, unified, and coherent	Remains on topic	Occasionally drifts off topic Some consistency on topic	Rambles from idea to idea
Organization and structure	Clear and effective transitions Has well- and evenly developed introduction, body, and conclusion, all of which catch reader's attention	Organization apparent, with some flaws Uses transitions Topic sentences present Has well-developed introduction, body, and conclusion but may be uneven	Organization apparent, with gaps and flaws Some transitions Some use of topic sentences Has introduction, body, and conclusion	Little or no order No transitions No topic sentences
Language control	Sentences varied and effective Few, if any, grammatical errors Little use of "being" verbs Rich and varied word choice	Some sentence variation Some errors in mechanics Some use of "being" verbs	Simple sentences used Errors in mechanics and spelling impede understanding Frequent use of "being" verbs	Simple sentences and fragments Major spelling and mechanical problems Very minimal word choice
Development of storyline	Storyline is superior	Storyline is apparent	Storyline has gaps	No storyline

Standard: Employ wide range of strategies in writing and use different writing-process elements appropriately to communicate with different audiences for variety of purposes

Persuasive Writing Rubric (First Draft)

Criteria	4 Exceeds Standard	3 Meets Standard	2 Is Below Standard	1 Does Not Meet Standard
Stay on topic	Presents convincing reasons in logical, unified manner Persuades convincingly	Remains on topic Response is consistent Persuades adequately	Addresses position and provides reasons Occasionally drifts from position/reasons	Addresses topic/purpose in skeletal or general manner Drifts from topic/purpose (why to how-to) Information does not support position Responses are not persuasive
Organization and structure	Clear sense of order and completeness Effective use of transitional elements Consistent organizational strategy evident Has introduction, body, and conclusion Gives at least four reasons in body paragraphs	Generally well-organized and clear enough to understand reasons presented Transition from one thought to another Has introduction, body, and conclusion Gives at least three reasons in body paragraphs	Has introduction and conclusion Organization apparent Some gaps, rambling, and inconsistencies	Lacks connection between responses

(continued on next page)

Persuasive Writing Rubric (First Draft) *(continued)*

Criteria	4 Exceeds Standard	3 Meets Standard	2 Is Below Standard	1 Does Not Meet Standard
Language control	Consistent control of language Few, if any, errors Varied sentence construction, including compound and complex sentences	Exhibits control of language Some errors slightly interrupt flow of language Some variations in sentence structure Complete sentences	Awkward or simple sentences Many errors in spelling, capitalization, and punctuation do not significantly affect understanding	Brief phrases Sentence fragments Illogical, confusing sentences Repeated errors in spelling and word choice
Support and elaboration	Specific and well-elaborated reasons that are clear and convincing Rich, unusual, and/or vivid word choice Exhibits three or more types of elaboration	Elaboration may support one fully developed reason or lengthy set of less-developed ideas Effective word choice Exhibits at least two types of elaboration	Some elaboration and/or extension of reasons Number of specific reasons provided Limited word choice	Insufficient elaboration to support position Brief list of non-specific and unelaborated reasons Minimal word choice

Standard: Employ wide range of strategies in writing and use different writing-process elements appropriately to communicate with different audiences for variety of purposes

Persuasive Writing Rubric (Final Draft)

	4	3	2	1
Criterion	**Exceeds Standard**	**Meets Standard**	**Is Below Standard**	**Does Not Meet Standard**
Mechanics, grammar, and conventions	Capitalization, punctuation, and spelling are acceptable for publication Virtually always has subject/verb agreement	Minor revisions to capitalization, punctuation, and spelling Punctuation needed Usually has subject/verb agreement	Some errors in capitalization, punctuation, and spelling Some mistakes in subject/verb agreement Some sentence fragments	Major errors in capitalization, punctuation, and spelling Incomplete sentences
Fluency *	250+	150–250	100–150	0–100

* These figures represent an approximate number of words occurring in papers with these scores. However, the focus should be on developing and elaborating ideas and not on counting words.

From *Meeting Standards & Raising Test Scores*, aha! Process, Inc.: www.ahaprocess.com

Study Tools

Mental Model for Research Calendar

Research Calendar

March 1 Library	March 2 Library	March 3 Library	March 4 Library	March 5 Library
March 8	March 9	March 10 10 source cards due	March 11	March 12
March 15	March 16	March 17 Outline due	March 18	March 19
March 22	March 23	March 24	March 25	March 26
March 29	March 30	March 31	April 1	April 2
April 5	April 6	April 7	April 8 Rough draft due	April 9
April 19	April 20	April 21	April 22 Final draft due	April 23

Mental Model for Research Calendar

STEP SHEET

Use this mental model to plan term papers.

1. Write down the steps necessary to complete the research paper.

2. Sketch a calendar showing all dates from the present to the deadline date.

3. Write "turn in research paper" in the deadline date.

4. Decide which would be the last step to be completed and determine how many days would be needed to complete this step. Count backward from the due date and write this step on the calendar on a date that would allow adequate time.

5. Continue working in reverse order, allowing adequate time for each step.

6. Adjust times, if necessary, to begin on the present day.

7. Compare your progress with your planning calendar as you complete each step.

8. Check off each step as completed.

Mental Model for Responding to
Open-Response Questions:
U R TOPS

U R TOPS

U	UNDERLINE	UNDERLINE or highlight key words, ideas, power verbs, and important information.
R	READ	READ everything twice before you start to answer. Read charts, diagrams, and maps, then reread the question.
T	TOPIC	Create a TOPIC SENTENCE that clearly states your position, decision, or starts your answer.
O	ORGANIZE	ORGANIZE your thoughts to answer the question. Be clear, concise, and to the point.
P	PART	Look for specific PARTS to be answered. Label each part with a number.
S	SUPPORT	SUPPORT your answer with facts, figures, or statements from what is given.

STEP SHEET

1. Study the mental model to determine the meaning of each step of the U R TOPS process.

2. Follow each step of the mental model to answer *Open-Response Questions*.

3. Put a check over the letters of the U R TOPS steps as you complete them.

4. Write your response.

Mental Model for Open-Response Questions: Quest

The Problem:

Open	**R**esponse	**Q**uestions

Essay questions simply require you to remember what has been taught and discussed in class and give that information back. Open-response questions, on the other hand, require you to apply your knowledge to situations that have not been discussed in class.

The Solution:

Open the topic	**R**esponse requirements	**Q**uest for information

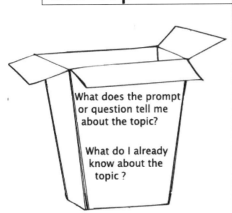

What does the prompt or question tell me about the topic?

What do I already know about the topic?

1. **What do I have to do?**
   List?
   Explain?
   Compare?
   Contrast?
   Describe?

2. **How many questions or question parts are there?**

How can I apply this topic to other things?

What experiences have I had with this?

What are three examples?

What real-life situations relate to this topic?

How can I support my answer?

Mental Model for Open-Response Questions: Quest

Standard: Apply wide range of strategies to comprehend, interpret, evaluate, and appreciate texts

STEP SHEET

Understanding the Mental Model

1. Read the *Problem* portion of the mental model, paying close attention to the meaning of ORQ (**O**pen-**R**esponse **Q**uestions).

2. Study the paragraph that explains the difference between essays and open-response questions.

3. Read the *Solution* portion of the mental model, paying close attention to the meaning of ORQ (**O**pen the topic, **R**esponse requirements, and **Q**uest for information).

Using the Mental Model

1. **Study Step 1**: Open the topic ...
   Jot down key words that describe the topic or question.

2. **Study Step 2**: Response requirements ...
   Identify all the parts of the questions and list them separately.

3. **Study Step 3**: Quest for information ...
   Jot down words that symbolize personal experiences, examples, applications, real-life situations, and other topics related to each response requirement.

4. Write your response.

www.ahaprocess.com

Mental Model for Reading Strategy

Standard: **Apply wide range of strategies to comprehend, interpret, evaluate, and appreciate texts**

1. Box in and read the title.
2. Trace and number the paragraphs.
3. Stop and think at the end of each paragraph to identify a key point.
4. Circle the key word or write the key point in the margin.
5. Read the questions.
6. Prove your answer; locate the paragraph where the answer is found.
7. Mark or write your answer.

1.

2.

3. **S T**

4.

5.

6. **P #**

7.

Mental Model for Reading Strategy

Standard: **Apply wide range of strategies to comprehend, interpret, evaluate, and appreciate texts.**

STEP SHEET

Use this mental model as a strategy for engaging with reading material and locating information in the material.

1. Read each step of the mental model.

2. Complete each step of the mental model in the sequence listed.

3. Practice each step many times prior to taking a reading test.

aha! Process, Inc.
P.O. Box 727, Highlands, TX 77562
(800) 424-9484; fax: (281) 426-5600
store@ahaprocess.com

www.ahaprocess.com

ORDER FORM

Please send me:

_____ COPY/COPIES of *Mental Models for English/Language Arts: Grades 1–6* Workbook

BOOKS: $10.00/each + $4.50 first book, plus $2.00 each additional book (shipping/handling)

UPS SHIP-TO ADDRESS (no post office boxes, please):

NAME _____

ORGANIZATION _____

ADDRESS _____

_____

PHONE(S) _____

E-MAIL ADDRESS(ES) _____

_____

METHOD OF PAYMENT:

PURCHASE ORDER # _____
PLEASE NOTE: Signed copy of purchase order must be submitted with completed order form.

CREDIT CARD TYPE _____ EXP _____

CREDIT CARD # _____

CHECK $ _____ CHECK # _____

SUBTOTAL $ _____

SHIPPING $ _____

SALES TAX $ _____ 6.25% IN TEXAS

TOTAL $ _____

More eye-openers at ...
www.ahaprocess.com

- **If you are interested in more information regarding seminars or training, we invite you to visit our website at www.ahaprocess.com.**

- **Join our aha! Process News List!**
  Receive the latest income and poverty statistics *free* when you join! Then receive periodic news and updates, recent articles written by Dr. Payne, and more!

- **Register for Dr. Payne's U.S. National Tour**

- **Visit our online store**
  - Books
  - Videos
  - Workshops

- **Additional programs/video series offered by aha! Process, Inc. include:**
  - *A Framework for Understanding Poverty*
  - *Meeting Standards & Raising Test Scores—When You Don't Have Much Time or Money*
  - *Tucker Signing Strategies for Reading*

- **For a complete listing of products, please visit www.ahaprocess.com**